SWEDEN
LA SUEDE · SCHWEDEN

SWEDEN

LA SUEDE · SCHWEDEN

———— ✳ ————

A Book of Photographs

with an Introduction by

IAN RODGER

———— ✳ ————

SPRING BOOKS · LONDON

Published by

SPRING BOOKS

SPRING HOUSE · SPRING PLACE · LONDON NW5

Printed in Czechoslovakia

T 726

CONTENTS

INTRODUCTION
BY IAN RODGER

PLATES
TABLEAUX   TAFELN

INDEX AND ACKNOWLEDGEMENTS

INTRODUCTION

Sweden is a country at rest. In a restless world a calm and peaceful place tends to be dismissed as dull and uninteresting. It is widely believed by people who have never travelled North that Sweden is dull and that there is a distressing coldness to be found in the land and in the people. The winter is of course severe and it deadens and numbs. But the summer can be like a dream of summer. The sun shines far longer and more brilliantly than it does on the shores of the Mediterranean. Burning in an endlessly pale blue sky, it shines with a sparkle and a clarity that makes the country a photographer's paradise. The lakes and the great forests drain the water from the air so that there is little glare and one does not need to squint or to strain the eyes. One can see great distances in Sweden. The eye is trained by the air and the ever rolling landscape to open wide. One does not look at Sweden. One gazes at it. It is a land that invites the eye of the dreamer and of the poet. It contains the essence of the meaning of tranquillity.

Tranquillity is not only a matter of climate. As soon as one arrives in Sweden one is aware that here is a country in which things are ordered and arranged in good time. This leisured orderliness has something to do with the fact that the Swedes know that they have ample time and space for whatever they wish to undertake but it is also the fruit of a long peace. The Swedish army, which was formerly the terror of Northern Europe, has not left the country since the beginning of the nineteenth century. It played a minor part in the War of Liberation against Napoleon under the command of Bernadotte, a former general of Bonaparte, who, as Charles XIV Johann, became king of Sweden. Considering neutrality more far-sighted and more advantageous he withdrew from the war. Since that triumph of good sense the Swedes have steadfastly opposed any attempt at embroiling them in war. Many less fortunate nations have accused them in jealousy of being cowardly, but it takes courage to maintain such a policy. The seeds of this policy of neutrality were sown in the years that followed the brilliant campaigns of Charles XII at the beginning of the eighteenth century. Though the young soldier King and his Scottish mercenary generals, whose descendants still own some of the great estates in the country, won victory after victory, their conquests were Pyrrhic and when the wars came to an end the country had lost three out of every four of the men who had marched from the land at the beginning of the wars. The country's economy was ruined and the Swedes realised that war does not pay. They therefore embarked on a policy of peace which they have maintained to the present day.

This policy has had its effects both internally and externally. The long years of slow and leisured development have given them a prosperity and a standard of comfort which makes them a little smug. Like the English, the Swedes tend to talk about the Continent as if they did not belong to it. Geographically Sweden is of course more a part of the continent of Europe than Britain, but the Swedes feel that the Baltic and the long spine of mountains which separates them from Norway make their country into an island. Even in the years when they sent armies to pillage Russia, Poland and Germany, the heart of the country around Stockholm was never invaded and though the southern provinces were occupied by the Danes for two centuries, no foreign army approached or entered the capital. Sweden is therefore unique in being the only country in Europe that has never known subjugation. The essence of being Swedish has therefore been preserved first by the geographic accident which made her militarily difficult to subdue and second by the policy which was adopted when her own military strength failed and it was clear that warlike policies might place her at the mercy of her enemies. The people who now live in the centrally heated apartments of modern Sweden are therefore the direct and pure descendants of the people who moved North at the time of Tacitus to cut their living from the forests.

The sense of this continuity is very strong in the provinces around Stockholm. Apart from the clearing of buildings to make way for more modern ones, there has been none of the destruction which has made towns in other parts of Europe so desolate. The towns that lie on the shores of Lake Mälar were born in the years of the great Viking expeditions which brought back gold and silver from Istanbul. With the discovery of the great deposits of iron and copper in Middle Sweden these towns became centres of importance in the Middle Ages. Some of them like Birka, which was once the largest commercial city in Scandinavia, have died and others like Strängnäs and Sigtuna are now sleepy cathedral towns with artists' and writers' colonies. But some of them like Västerås and Eskilstuna have kept pace with industrial development. Even these so-called industrial towns have a charm that is unexpected if one happens to come from England, France or Germany. A town like Södertälje, for example, which lies to the south of Stockholm, where it is said that the best Swedish is spoken, is the home of one of Sweden's car manufacturing firms. It is a rail centre and is cut by a canal. But the modern apartments grow up beside the eighteenth century timber houses and in the centre, beside the bus station, there is a runestone that was placed there by a Södertälje man a thousand years ago. Runestones are quite a feature of the Södermannland and Uppland landscape as are also the hundreds of little churches that date from the conversion of Sweden to Christianity.

If one comes from a country where time is measured by the dates of wars and battles, one finds an enchantment in the small villages of Sweden where one can know with certainty that nothing violent has happened for almost a thousand years. It is only in the museums of Stockholm or at places like Mariefred, where the great round fortress of Gripsholm looms over the waters of Lake Mälar, that one comes across the memory of spilt blood. Gripsholm is certainly worth a visit. It was once the home of the Vasas, that extraordinary family who gave the country the warrior genius of Gustavus Adolphus and the intellectual genius of the first blue-stocking, Queen Christina. It was here that the mad king Erik XIV was imprisoned in an octagonal tower and it is here that one can see not only the portraits of Swedish kings but some little known studies of the young Mary, Queen of Scots, of Elizabeth of England and of Cromwell. As is the custom of the Swedish museums, the castle is furnished even to the detail of putting soap and towels in the maids' bedrooms so that the visitor feels that he is walking round a place which has only been temporarily vacated by the original occupants. It was from this castle that the Vasas first subdued the surrounding country and commanded the western approaches to Stockholm.

The eastern approach to Stockholm has never needed very much defending. Stockholm stands at the end of Lake Mälar. To the east of the city lies one of the most beautiful archipelagoes in the world. The channels between the thousands of tree-covered islands wind tortuously for forty miles from the sea to the capital.

Stockholm's Old Town, which is dominated by the spires of the churches and the great block of the Palladian style Royal Palace, is bunched on the three islands that separate the archipelago system from Lake Mälar. The town that has spread during the last fifty years beyond the immediate north and south banks is linked by tunnels and bridges which leap across the minor waterways and the smaller islands. The decaying Old Town which contains restaurants and inns, often with cellars dating from the Middle Ages, contrasts sharply with the bridges and buildings of the twentieth century. In Stockholm one is never really out of touch with the country and nature and yet in Stockholm one is also aware that a modern city is like a beautiful piece of machinery.

The thought that modern buildings and machinery can be beautiful may strike anyone who has never been to Sweden as rather unfelicitous. In Sweden such an axiom is undisputed and completely accepted. It is accepted because the Swedes believe in a kind of planning which takes account of every eventuality. They have time on their side so they do not hurry or skimp their work. They also have plenty of space. Sweden is one of the few countries in Europe where one can be aware of the land's vastness. It is twice the size of Great Britain and yet it contains only seven and a half million people of whom one million live in and around Stockholm. It takes more than thirty hours to travel by fast train from Malmö in the south to the mining town of Kiruna which is north of the Arctic Circle. As the train strikes north beyond Stockholm it enters a sea of trees that cover the rolling post-glacial landscape. In this rolling sea of trees — broken only occasionally by small lakes — towns and villages and the great engineering projects of twentieth century man are lost and swallowed up.

Even when industry is concentrated, the prospect pleases. The copper and iron mining and smelting began in neo-prehistoric times, but it remained what might be called a cottage industry until the end of the last century. Though Sweden possesses great mineral wealth she suffers from a lack of coal. If coal had existed in large quantities her history might have been different. But the lack of coal prevented the early industrialisation which has turned some parts of Britain, France and Germany into blackened smoky deserts. It postponed the development of her cities and maintained the continuance of a predominantly agricultural community until the end of the nineteenth century. When industrial processes had been developed after messy experiment in Britain and Germany, Swedish industrialisation began. Industrialists were thus able to put up their factories in one piece and at one go. The squalor and untidiness which is the distressing product of early industrial experiment in other countries is therefore missing in Sweden. A port like Gothenburg, or a commercial city like Malmö, is a beautiful thing to look at. One lingers in Sweden's industrial cities because they are attractive and pleasant to live in.

The visual appeal of Sweden should be evident from the photographs in this book. There is however, something more in Sweden than the attractiveness of things seen. The Swedish people are a lonely people. They are for the most part only one generation away from the life of the deep country and from the centuries of forest isolation. This makes them shy in a way that sometimes makes foreigners mistakenly think of them as aloof or proud. It also makes them naïve and almost pathetically interested in the world outside and in the opinion that foreigners have of them. If they overcome their shyness, they will deluge the visitor with an alarming flood of questions. Envy has inspired many foreigners to write and say things about the Swedes and their country which are not wholly true. They are extremely sensitive to criticism and need desperately to know that they are doing the right thing. The prosperity and comfort which has been the fruit of their good sense in foreign policy makes them feel cut off from people in less fortunate countries and sometimes gives them a sense of guilt. This is unfortunate for, without realising it, they have created the blueprint for the future. It would be silly to maintain that this blueprint does not contain disadvantages.

The concentration on the pursuits of peace has raised the status of the men of peace and the social policies of the government have placed a premium on intelligence rather than on birth or wealth. But this concentration does of course bring in its train a certain solemnity and lack of vitality. Though the foreigner is pleased to notice an absence of vulgarity in Swedish life there is also a lack of pulse. The man who wants to spend his holidays in night clubs is well advised to steer clear of Sweden. There is nothing jazzy or raucous about a Swedish holiday.

There is however an enormous charm and the country's size provides tremendous contrasts. While the inhabitant of Malmö or Stockholm engages in a life that is similar to that enjoyed in the rest of urban Europe, the Lappish people who live in the Northern provinces still herd reindeer as they have done for centuries. Even in the cities the remembrance of country ways and customs is still strong and I shall always remember the incongruous sight of the tar and pitch torches that greet the New Year flaming from the balconies of the centrally heated apartments in Stockholm. At times of festival, the Swedes shake off their newly found urbanity and revert to country ways. At Midsummer for example they seem to disappear from the cities and the foreigner will be lucky if he can find them. They will be dancing round the Midsummer Pole as their ancestors did in the years before Christianity came North. At such times one realises that they have not lost as much through planning and urban development as many superficial observers would think that they had.

The Swedish housewife may enjoy millionaire conditions in her modern kitchen but she still spends hours preparing traditional fare. The supermarket and the automat are part of Swedish life but there is still no such thing as a standardised loaf of bread. There are countless variations in the taste and texture of Swedish loaves. There are many ways of serving and preserving fish. Though there is a high salt content in food in the North owing to the absence of mineral salts in the melted snow water, there is little in Swedish cuisine that should frighten the foreigner. The squeamish may wish to avoid rotted herring which is considered a great delicacy but the gourmet should mark the last two weeks in August as the time for the crayfish which is very nearly an object of worship.

Worship may be too big a word for the crayfish but it is certainly not too large for the feeling that one develops for the Swedish landscape. There is something in the Swedish summer sky which is suggestive of eternity. I have experienced moments when I have felt that Sweden is almost too beautiful. The landscape never shocks or hinders the view. There is always the hint of something further beyond the immediately seen horizon. Even in the cities there is the scent of the pines and the echo of the roar of the seas of forests. One feels relaxed and free. One also shares for a little while the Swedish experience, the experience of knowing that man is terribly alone and that he is much smaller than his shouts often proclaim. There is something humbling about the Swedish landscape, something at the same time relaxing and inspiring. There is something in it that makes one cry out at so much beauty and yet makes it very difficult to put into words. A country like Sweden does not really need words. It needs seeing. It hushes the mouth and opens the eyes.

INTRODUCTION

La Suède est un pays en repos. Dans notre monde agité on est tenté de classer une contrée calme et paisible comme ennuyeuse et sans intérêt. Souvent ceux qui n'ont jamais voyagé dans le nord, considèrent que la Suède est un pays morne où une froideur désolante règne sur la terre et ses habitants. Certes, l'hiver est rigoureux, il assoupit et engourdit. Mais l'été peut être idéal. Le soleil y luit plus longuement et avec plus de furie que sur le rivage de la Méditerrannée. Brûlant dans un ciel bleu pâle sans fin, il brille d'un éclat et d'une clarté tels que ce pays est le paradis du photographe. Les lacs et les grandes forêts captent l'humidité de l'air, si bien que l'œil peu ébloui ne louche ni ne se fatigue. En Suède la vue s'étend au loin. L'œil s'habitue grâce à l'air et au paysage ondulant à demeurer grand ouvert. On ne regarde pas la Suède. On la contemple. C'est un pays qui flatte l'œil du rêveur et du poète. Il possède l'essence de ce que représente la tranquillité.

La tranquillité ne dépend seulement du climat. Aussitôt arrivé en Suède, on s'aperçoit que tout s'y prépare et s'y ordonne à temps. Cette manière nonchalante de vivre est due en partie au fait que le Suédois sait qu'il a tout le temps et l'espace voulus pour accomplir ses projets et elle est également le fruit d'une paix prolongée. L'armée suédoise qui faisait autrefois règner la terreur en Europe du Nord, n'est pas sortie de son pays depuis le début du 19ème siècle. Elle ne joua qu'un moindre rôle dans la Guerre de Libération contre Napoléon, sous le commandement de Bernadotte, un ancien général de Bonaparte qui, sous le titre de Charles XIV Johann, devint roi de Suède. Convaincu que la neutralité serait plus avantageuse pour le présent et l'avenir du pays, il se retira de la guerre. Depuis cette victoire du bon sens, les Suédois se sont fermement opposés à toute tentative d'être entrainés dans la guerre. Bien des nations moins fortunées les ont, par jalousie, accusés d'être lâches, mais il faut au contraire du courage pour maintenir une telle ligne de conduite. La semence de cette politique de neutralité avait été répandue dans les années qui suivirent les éclatantes campagnes de Charles XII au début du dix-huitième siècle. Bien que le jeune roi soldat et ses généraux mercenaires écossais, dont les descendants possèdent encore maintenant quelques grandes propriétés dans le pays, gagnassent victoire sur victoire, leurs conquêtes furent à la Pyrrhus et lorsque la guerre se termina, le pays avait perdu les trois quarts des hommes qui avaient quitté la terre au début de la guerre. L'économie du pays était ruineé et les Suédois se rendirent compte que la guerre ne paie pas. Ils s'embarquèrent donc dans une politique de paix qu'ils ont maintenue jusqu'à nos jours.

Cette politique eut des répercussions aussi bien à l'intérieur qu'à l'extérieur. Les longues années d'un développement lent et paisible ont donné au pays une prospérité et un niveau de confort qui rend les Suédois quelque peu satisfaits d'eux-mêmes. Comme les Anglais, ils ont tendance à parler du Continent comme si la Suède n'en faisait pas partie. Géographiquement parlant, la Suède fait naturellement plus partie du continent européen que la Grande-Bretagne, mais les Suédois ont l'impression que la Baltique et la longue crête de montagnes qui les sépare de la Norvège font de leur pays une île. Même dans les années pendant lesquelles ils envoyaient des armées piller la Russie, la Pologne et l'Allemagne, le cœur du pays, autour de Stockholm, ne fut jamais envahi et bien que les provinces du sud aient été occupées par les Danois pendant deux siècles, aucune armée étrangère n'est entrée dans la capitale ni même s'en est approchée. Aussi la Suède est-elle le seul pays d'Europe qui n'a jamais connu d'assujettissement. Le vrai caractère de la Suède a donc été conservé, d'une part par le hasard géographique qui en fait un pays militairement difficile à soumettre et d'autre part par la ligne de conduite qu'elle a adoptée lorsque sa force militaire fléchit et qu'elle comprit qu'une politique de guerre pourrait la mettre à la merci de ses ennemis. Les habitants actuels des appartements à chauffage central de la Suède moderne sont donc les descendants directs et purs de ceux qui, au temps de Tacite, montaient vers le nord pour tailler leur vie dans les forêts.

Cette continuité est très apparente dans les provinces aux alentours de Stockholm. A part la démolition de constructions anciennes remplacées par des immeubles plus modernes, elles n'ont connu aucune de ces destructions qui ont ravagé les villes d'autres contrées européennes. Les villes situées sur les rives du Lac Mälar naquirent lors des grandes expéditions des Vikings, qui ramenaient or et argent d'Istamboul. Avec la découverte des grands gisements de fer et de cuivre de la Suède Centrale, ces villes devinrent, au Moyen-Age, des centres importants. Quelques unes, telles que Birka, qui fut la plus grande ville commerciale de la Suède, ont disparu ; d'autres, telles que Strängnäs et Sigtuna sont maintenant des villes episcopales endormies, où vivent des colonies d'artistes et d'écrivains. Mais certaines d'entre elles, telles que Västerås et Eskilstuna, ont suivi l'évolution du développement industriel. Même celles qui sont considérées cités industrielles possèdent un charme inattendu pour quiconque vient d'Angleterre, de France ou d'Allemagne. Une ville comme Södertälje, par exemple, au sud de Stockholm, où dit-on la langue suédoise est la mieux parlée, est le siège d'une des entreprises automobiles de Suède. C'est un centre ferroviaire traversé par un canal. Mais les bâtiments modernes y voisinent avec les maisons de bois du dix-huitième siècle, et au coeur de la ville près de la station d'autobus, se trouve une pierre runique placée là par un habitant de Södertälje, il y a environ mille ans. Les pierres runiques sont caractéristiques du Södermanland et du Uppland aussi bien que les centaines de petites églises qui datent du temps de la conversion de la Suède au christianisme.

Si vous venez d'un pays où le temps se mesure en dates de guerres et de batailles, vous serez enchanté par les petits villages de Suède où vous pourrez être certain qu'aucune violence n'a eu lieu depuis près de mille années. Ce n'est que dans les musées de Stockholm, ou par exemple à Mariefred, et sa grande forteresse ronde de Gripsholm qui s'élève dans le brouillard au dessus des eaux du Lac Mälar, que vous rencontrerez le souvenir du sang versé. Gripsholm vaut certainement une visite. Ce fut jadis le foyer des Vasa, cette famille extraordinaire qui donna au pays le génie guerrier de Gustave Adolphe et le génie intellectuel du premier bas-bleu, la Reine Christine. C'est ici que le roi fou Eric XIV fut emprisonné dans une tour octogonale et c'est ici que vous pourrez voir non seulement les portraits des rois de Suède, mais aussi quelques études peu connues de la jeune Mary, Reine d'Ecosse, d'Elisabeth d'Angleterre et de Cromwell. Selon l'usage des musées suédois, le château est entièrement meublé jusque dans les moindres détails, tels savon et serviettes de toilette dans les chambres de bonnes, de sorte que le visiteur a la sensation de visiter une demeure délaissée temporairement par ses premiers occupants. C'est de ce château que les Vasas soumirent pour la première fois le pays environnant et qu'ils maîtrisèrent les voies d'accès ouest de Stockholm.

L'accès est de Stockholm n'a jamais eu grand besoin de défense. Stockholm est situé au bout du Lac Mälar. A l'est de la ville se trouve l'un des plus beaux archipels du monde. Entre des milliers d'îles boisées les canaux sillonnent les soixante kilomètres qui séparent la capitale de la mer.

Le Vieux Stockholm, dominé par les flèches de ses églises et par la grande masse du Palais Royal du style de Palladio, se serre sur les trois îles qui séparent l'archipel du Lac Mälar. La ville, qui, au cours des dernières cinquante années, s'est étalée au delà des rives nord et sud les plus proches, y est reliée par des tunnels et des ponts qui franchissent les voies d'eau secondaires et les petites îles. La Vieille Ville en son déclin, où restaurants et auberges possèdent souvent des caves moyenâgeuses, offre un contraste frappant avec les ponts et les immeubles du vingtième siècle. A Stockholm, vous ne perdrez jamais contact avec la campagne et la nature, et pourtant, à Stockholm, vous réaliserez qu'une ville moderne est comme une magnifique machine.

La pensée que des immeubles et des machines modernes peuvent être beaux semblera peut-être fort peu heureuse à quiconque n'a jamais été en Suède. Dans ce pays, un tel axiome ne soulève aucune discussion et est tout a fait accepté. Il est accepté parce que les Suédois croient en une planification qui tient compte de toute éventualité. Ils ont le temps pour eux, aussi ne se pressent-ils pas et ne mesurent-ils pas leur peine. Ils ont également beaucoup d'espace. La Suède est l'un des rares pays d'Europe dont on peut réaliser l'immensité. Elle est deux fois plus étendue que la Grande-Bretagne et cependant sa population ne compte que sept millions et demi d'habitants dont un million vit à Stockholm et ses environs. Il faut plus de trente heures de voyage en train rapide pour arriver de Malmö, qui se trouve au sud, à la ville minière de Kiruna qui est située au nord du Cercle Polaire. En s'avançant vers le nord, au delà de Stockholm, le train pénètre dans la mer d'arbres qui recouvre un paysage ondulé de la période post-glaciaire. Dans cette mer mouvante d'arbres — parsemée seulement de temps à autre par de petits lacs — les villes et les villages, ainsi que les grandes constructions de l'homme du vingtième siècle, sont perdus et engloutis.

Même lorsque l'industrie est concentrée, la vue reste agréable. L'extraction et la fonte du cuivre et du fer remontent aux temps néo-préhistoriques, mais ils sont restés pour ainsi dire une industrie artisanale jusqu'à la fin du siècle dernier. Bien que la Suède soit très riche en minerais, elle souffre d'un manque de charbon. Si elle en avait possédé en grandes quantités son histoire aurait pu être différente. Mais le manque de charbon fit obstacle à l'industrialisation rapide qui transforma certaines régions de la Grande-Bretagne, de France et d'Allemagne en des déserts noircis de fumée. Il a retardé le développement de ses villes et a maintenu la continuité d'une communauté à prédominance agricole jusqu'à la fin du dix-neuvième siècle. Ce n'est que lorsque les procédés industriels furent développés après l'expérience désordonnée de Grande-Bretagne et d'Allemagne que l'industrialisation suédoise prit le départ. Les industriels ont ainsi pu monter leurs usines d'une seule pièce et d'un seul coup. C'est pourquoi on ne trouve en Suède ni la malpropreté ni le désordre, résultats affligeants des premières expériences industrielles d'autres pays. Un port tel que Gothenbourg ou une ville commerciale telle que Malmö vous offre un spectacle de toute beauté. Vous vous attarderez dans les villes industrielles de Suède parce qu'elles sont séduisantes et et qu'il y est fait bon vivre.

Le spectacle séduisant de la Suède devrait ressortir avec évidence des photos de ce livre. Mais il y a en Suède plus que l'attrait des beautés visuelles. Les suédois sont des gens solitaires. La majorité d'entre eux n'est séparée que par une génération de la vie dans la campagne éloignée et de siècles d'isolement dans les forêts. Aussi sont-ils timides d'une façon qui fait parfois penser à tort aux étrangers qu'ils sont distants et fiers. Celà les rend aussi naïfs et presque pathétiquement intéressés au monde extérieur et à l'opinion des étrangers sur eux. S'ils surmontent leur timidité, ils inondent le visiteur d'un flot inquiétant de questions. La jalousie a fait beaucoup d'étrangers écrire et dire, sur les Suédois et sur leur pays, des choses qui ne sont pas rigoureusement vraies. Les Suédois sont extrêmement sensibles à la critique et ont un besoin désespéré de savoir qu'ils font ce qui se doit. La prospérité et le confort, fruits de leur bon sens en politique étrangère, leur donne le sentiment d'être coupés des peuples de pays moins fortunés et parfois leur donnent un sentiment de culpabilité. Ceci est dommage car, sans s'en rendre compte, ils ont créé un modèle pour l'avenir. Il serait néanmoins stupide d'affirmer que ce modèle est sans inconvénients.

La concentration des efforts à la recherche de la paix a donné naissance à 'l'homme de la paix', et la politique sociale du gouvernement a donné plus de valeur à l'intelligence qu'à la naissance ou la richesse. Mais cette concentration entraîne évidemment une certaine solennité et un manque de vitalité. Bien que l'étranger note avec plaisir l'absence de vulgarité dans la vie suédoise, il y a aussi un certain manque de vie. Celui qui veut passer ses vacances dans des cabarets ferait bien de rester loin de la Suède. Pas de jazz ni de voix eraillées durant des vacances suédoises.

Un grand charme s'émane du pays et son étendue vous offre des contrastes frappants. Alors que les habitants de Malmö ou de Stockholm mènent une vie semblable à celle du reste des villes d'Europe, les Lapons des provinces du nord élèvent encore des rennes comme ils l'ont fait pendant des siècles. Même dans les villes le souvenir des us et coutumes campagnards reste vivant, et je me rappelerai toujours la vue surprenante des torches de poix et de goudron saluant la Nouvelle Année aux balcons des appartements à chauffage central de Stockholm. Aux moments des fêtes, les Suédois se débarassent de leur urbanité nouvellement acquise et retrouvent leurs manières paysannes. En plein été, par exemple, ils semblent disparaître des villes et l'étranger aura de la chance s'il peut les trouver. Ils seront en train de danser autour du mât de la Saint-Jean comme le firent leurs ancêtres avant l'arrivée du christianisme dans le nord. C'est alors qu'on réalisera que la planification et le développement urbain ne leur ont pas fait perdre autant que les observateurs superficiels le pensent.

Dans sa cuisine moderne, la ménagère suédoise peut jouir d'un cadre semblable à celles de millionnaires, cependant elle passera des heures à préparer des plats traditionnels. Le super-marché et le restaurant automatique font partie de la vie suédoise, mais il n'y a pas encore de pain standard. Les pains suédois varient à l'infini de part leurs goûts et consistences. Nombreuses sont les façons de servir et de conserver le poisson. Bien que la cuisine du nord soit très salée en raison de l'absence de sels minéraux dans l'eau provenant de la neige fondue, fort peu de plats suédois devraient inquiéter l'étranger. Les plus difficiles pourront peut-être éviter de manger le hareng pourri qui est considéré comme une grande délicatesse, mais le gourmet devrait marquer les dernières deux semaines du mois d'août par la dégustation des écrevisses, qui sont presque un objet de vénération.

Vénération peut être un mot trop fort pour l'écrevisse, il ne l'est certainement pas pour le sentiment que l'on éprouve pour le paysage suédois. Il y a quelque chose, dans le ciel d'été de la Suède, qui évoque l'idée d'éternité. Il m'est arrivé de penser par moments que la Suède est presque trop belle. Le paysage ne heurte jamais ni n'arrête jamais la vue. Il y a toujours la suggestion que quelque chose vous attend derrière l'horizon immédiat. Même dans les villes on trouve l'odeur des pins et l'écho mugissant des mers forestières. On se sent détendu et libre. On prend part un instant à l'expérience suédoise, à la connaissance du fait que l'homme est terriblement seul et qu'il est beaucoup plus petit qu'il ne le proclame souvent. Il y a quelque chose qui vous rend humble dans le paysage suédois, quelque chose qui tout à la fois vous repose et vous inspire. Il y a quelque chose dans ce paysage qui vous fait pousser des cris d'enthousiasme devant tant de beauté, mais qui se laisse difficilement exprimer par des mots. Un pays comme la Suède ne se décrit pas. Il faut le voir; alors la bouche se clôt et les yeux s'ouvrent tout grands.

EINLEITUNG

Schweden ist ein ausgeglichenes Land. In unserer rastlosen Welt neigt man dazu, einen ruhigen und friedlichen Ort als eintönig und uninteressant abzutun. Unter jenen, die nie den Norden bereist haben, besteht die weitverbreitete Meinung, daß Schweden langweilig sei und daß man im Land und bei seinen Leuten einer peinlichen Kälte begegne. Der Winter ist natürlich kalt; er stumpft die Gefühle ab und läßt alles erstarren. Der Sommer hingegen kann wie ein Traum sein. Die Sonne scheint wesentlich länger und strahlender als an den Gestaden des Mittelmeeres. Ihr gleißendes Licht funkelt so hell unter einem endlosen azurblauen Himmel, daß sich das Land in ein Paradies der Fotografen verwandelt. Die Seen und die großen Wälder entziehen der Luft das Wasser, so daß die Sonne nicht blendet und man weder blinzeln noch die Augen zusammenkneifen muß. Man kann in Schweden auf große Entfernungen sehen. Das Auge ist durch die Luft und die wellenförmige Landschaft daran gewöhnt, sich weit zu öffnen. Man blickt nicht auf Schweden, man starrt darauf. Es ist ein Land, das das Auge des Träumers und des Dichters einlädt; es enthält das Wesen dessen, was man unter Ruhe versteht.

Ruhe ist nicht nur Sache des Klimas. Kaum in Schweden angekommen, wird man sich bewußt, daß dies ein Land ist, in dem alles rechtzeitig eingerichtet und geregelt wird. Diese beschauliche Ordnungsliebe steht im Zusammenhang damit, daß die Schweden wissen, sie haben ausreichend Zeit und Raum für all ihre Vorhaben; sie ist jedoch auch das Ergebnis eines langanhaltenden Friedens. Die schwedischen Armeen, die einst der Schrecken Nordeuropas waren, haben das Land seit Beginn des neunzehnten Jahrhunderts nicht mehr verlassen. In den Freiheitskriegen gegen Napoleon spielten sie noch eine untergeordnete Rolle unter ihrem Feldherrn Bernadotte, dem einstigen General Bonapartes, der später als Karl XIV. Johann den schwedischen Thron bestieg. Da Bernadotte es für vorausschauender und vorteilhafter hielt, Neutralität zu wahren, zog er sich aus dem Krieg zurück. Seit diesem Sieg der Vernunft haben sich die Schweden standhaft jedem Versuch, sie in eine bewaffnete Auseinandersetzung zu verwickeln, widersetzt. Viele weniger glückliche Nationen haben sie aus Neid als Feiglinge bezeichnet, aber es erfordert ganz im Gegenteil Mut, eine solche Politik durchzuführen. Die Saat dieser Neutralitätspolitik wurde in den Jahren gesät, die den glänzenden Feldzügen Karls XII. zu Beginn des achtzehnten Jahrhunderts folgten. Wenn auch der junge Soldatenkönig und seine schottischen Söldnergeneräle, deren Nachkommen noch einige der großen Besitztümer des Landes innehaben, Sieg über Sieg errangen, so waren doch ihre Eroberungen Pyrrhussiege, und am Ende des Krieges hatte Schweden dreiviertel der Männer verloren, die zu Beginn in den Kampf gezogen waren. Die Wirtschaft des Landes war zerstört, und der Bevölkerung wurde klar, daß Kriege sich nicht bezahlt machen. Deshalb wandten die Schweden sich einer Politik des Friedens zu, die sie bis heute beibehalten haben.

Diese Politik hatte ihre Auswirkungen nach innen wie nach außen. Die langen Jahre langsamer und gemächlicher Entwicklung haben den Menschen Wohlstand und Behaglichkeit eingebracht, die sie ein wenig selbstzufrieden machen. Wie die Engländer, so haben auch die Schweden die Tendenz, über den Kontinent zu sprechen, als ob sie nicht zu ihm gehörten. Geographisch gesehen ist das Land eher ein Teil Europas als England, aber die Schweden fühlen sich durch die Ostsee und die lange Bergkette, die sie von Norwegen trennt, wie auf einer Insel. Selbst zu der Zeit, als sie Armeen aussandten, um Rußland, Polen und Deutschland zu plündern, wurde das Herzstück des Landes rund um Stockholm nie überfallen, und obwohl die südlichen Provinzen zwei Jahrhunderte lang von den Dänen besetzt waren, betrat keine fremde Armee je die Hauptstadt oder ihre Umgebung. Schweden ist daher das einzige Land Europas, das nie eine Unterjochung gekannt hat. So konnte die Nation ihre Eigenart bewahren: einerseits durch einen geographischen Zufall, der es schwierig machte, das Land militärisch zu unterwerfen, und andererseits durch die Politik, die angewandt wurde, als die militärische Stärke versagte und es klar war, daß eine Kriegspolitik das Land seinen Feinden ausliefern würde. Die Menschen, die heute in den zentralgeheizten Wohnungen des modernen Schweden leben, sind daher die direkten und reinen Nachkommen jener, die zur Zeit des Tacitus nach Norden zogen, um sich ihr Leben aus den Wäldern zu schlagen.

Das Bewußtsein dieser ununterbrochenen Entwicklung ist in den Provinzen rund um Stockholm sehr stark. Die Tatsache ausgenommen, daß alte Häuser neuen weichen mußten, gab es keine jener Zerstörungen, die die Städte in anderen Teilen Europas so trostlos machen. Die Siedlungen an den Ufern des Mälar-Sees sind in den Jahren der großen Züge der Wikinger entstanden, die Gold und Silber aus Istambul zurückbrachten. Mit der Entdeckung der ansehnlichen Eisen- und Kupferlager in Mittelschweden wurden diese Städte im Mittelalter zu bedeutenden Zentren. Einige von ihnen, wie Birka, das einst die größte Handelsstadt Skandinaviens war, sind untergegangen; andere, wie Strängnäs und Sigtuna, sind nun verschlafene Kirchenstädte mit Künstler- und Schriftstellerniederlassungen. Andere jedoch, wie Västerås und

Eskilstuna, haben mit der industriellen Entwicklung Schritt gehalten. Selbst diese sogenannten Industriestädte haben einen eigenartigen Reiz, der überraschend wirkt, wenn man von England Frankreich oder Deutschland kommt. Södertälje, zum Beispiel, das südlich von Stockholm liegt und von dem man sagt, daß dort das beste Schwedisch gesprochen wird, beherbergt eine von Schwedens Fahrzeugfabriken. Södertälje ist ein Bahnknotenpunkt und wird von einem Kanal durchschnitten. Die modernen Wohnungen wachsen neben Holzhäusern aus dem achtzehnten Jahrhundert in die Höhe, und im Zentrum, neben der Autobushaltestelle, steht ein Runenstein, der von einem Södertaler vor tausend Jahren dorthin gesetzt wurde. Runensteine sind eines der Merkmale der Landschaft Södermanland und des Hochlandes, so wie die Hunderte von kleinen Kirchen, die aus der Zeit stammen, da Schweden zum Christentum bekehrt wurde.

Wer aus einem Lande kommt, wo die Zeit nach Jahreszahlen von Kriegen und Kämpfen gemessen wird, ist entzückt über die kleinen Dörfer Schwedens, von denen man mit Sicherheit weiß, daß sich in ihnen seit beinahe tausend Jahren keine Gewalttat zugetragen hat. Einzig in den Museen von Stockholm oder an Orten wie Mariefred, wo die große runde Festung von Gripsholm über den Wassern des Mälar-Sees brütet, begegnet man der Erinnerung an vergossenes Blut. Gripsholm ist sicher einen Besuch wert. Es war einst das Heim der Wasa, dieses außergewöhnlichen Hauses, das dem Land den Kriegsgenius Gustav Adolf und das Genie der ersten gelehrten Frau, der Königin Christine, gab. Hier war auch der geisteskranke König Erich XIV. in einem achteckigen Turm eingeschlossen, und hier kann man neben Porträts der schwedischen Herrscher einige wenig bekannte Studien der jungen schottischen Königin Mary, Elisabeths von England und Cromwells sehen. Wie dies in den schwedischen Museen Sitte ist, enthält das Schloß eine bis in alle Einzelheiten vollständige Einrichtung, sogar Seife und Handtücher in den Schlafzimmern der Zofen hat man nicht vergessen, um bei dem Besucher das Gefühl zu erwecken, daß er einen Ort besucht, der nur vorübergehend von seinen eigentlichen Bewohnern verlassen wurde. Von diesem Schloß aus unterjochten die Wasa zuerst das umliegende Land, von hier aus beherrschten sie die westlichen Zufahrtsstraßen Stockholms.

Im Osten bedurfte Stockholm nie einer besonderen Verteidigung. Die Stadt liegt am Ende des Mälar-Sees. Östlich vorgelagert ist ihr eines der schönsten Inselgebiete der Welt. Die Kanäle zwischen den Tausenden waldbestandener Inseln schlängeln sich über eine Strecke von sechzig Kilometern zur Hauptstadt hin.

Stockholms Altstadt, die von den Kirchturmspitzen und dem großen Block des königlichen Palastes im Palladianischen Stil überragt wird, ist auf drei Inseln zusammengedrängt, die den Mälar-See von dem Inselmeer der Küste trennen. Die Stadt, die sich während der vergangenen fünfzig Jahre über die unmittelbaren Nord- und Südufer hinaus ausgedehnt hat, ist durch

Tunnel und Brücken verbunden, die sich über kleinere Wasserwege spannen und kleinere Inseln durchqueren. Die verfallene Altstadt, deren Restaurants und Gaststätten oft noch Keller aus dem Mittelalter besitzen, steht in scharfem Gegensatz zu den Brücken und Gebäuden des zwanzigsten Jahrhunderts. In Stockholm ist man nie wirklich außer Berührung mit dem Land und der Natur, und doch wird man hier gewahr, daß eine moderne Stadt einem prachtvollen Stück Technik gleicht.

Der Gedanke, daß neuzeitliche Gebäude und technische Anlagen schön sein können, mag jeden, der nie in Schweden gewesen ist, eher etwas unglücklich anmuten. Dort jedoch ist solch ein Grundsatz unbestritten und allgemein anerkannt. Er wird gebilligt, weil die Schweden an eine Art Planung glauben, die jedem Zufall Rechnung trägt. Sie haben die Zeit auf ihrer Seite; deshalb beeilen sie sich nicht und geizen nicht in ihrer Arbeit. Sie haben auch genügend Spielraum. Schweden ist einer der seltenen Staaten Europas, wo man sich der Ausdehnung des Landes bewußt wird. Es ist fast doppelt so groß wie Großbritannien und hat dennoch nur siebeneinhalb Millionen Einwohner, von denen eine Million in und rund um Stockholm lebt. Eine Reise mit einem Schnellzug von Malmö im Süden bis zur Bergwerksstadt Kiruna, die nördlich des Polarkreises liegt, dauert über dreißig Stunden. Wenn der Zug Stockholm verlassen hat und nach Norden eilt, dringt er in ein Meer von Bäumen ein, das die hügelige, von der Eiszeit geprägte Landschaft bedeckt. In diesem wogenden Wäldermeer, das nur ab und zu von kleinen Seen unterbrochen wird, verlieren sich die Städte und Dörfer und die großen Anlagen der Techniker des zwanzigsten Jahrhunderts.

Selbst jene Orte, in denen Industrieniederlassungen konzentriert sind, haben ein gefälliges Aussehen. Förderung und Schmelzen von Kupfer und Eisen gehen auf die späte Urzeit zurück; sie blieben jedoch bis Ende des vergangenen Jahrhunderts im handwerklichen Stadium. Obwohl Schweden reich an Bodenschätzen ist, fehlt ihm Kohle. Hätte es sie in großem Ausmaße besessen, so wäre vielleicht seine Geschichte anders verlaufen. Der Mangel an Kohle behinderte jedoch eine frühzeitige Industrialisierung, die manche Gegenden Großbritanniens, Frankreichs und Deutschlands in rauchgeschwärzte Öden verwandelt hat. Er schob die Entwicklung der Städte hinaus und führte zum Fortbestand einer vorwiegend landwirtschaftlichen Gemeinschaft bis Ende des neunzehnten Jahrhunderts. Die schwedische Industrialisierung begann erst, als der entsprechende Prozeß, nach ungeordneten Versuchen, in Großbritannien und Deutschland bereits angelaufen war. Die Unternehmer konnten daher ihre Fabriken zügig und mit einem Schlag aufbauen. Der Schmutz und die Unordnung, die das schmerzliche Ergebnis früher industrieller Versuche in anderen Ländern sind, fehlen darum in Schweden. Ein Hafen wie Göteborg oder eine Handelsstadt wie Malmö wirken ansprechend auf den Betrachter. Man verweilt in Schwedens Industriestädten, weil sie anziehend sind und man sich in ihnen wohlfühlt.

Der visuelle Reiz des Landes dürfte aus den Bildern dieses Buches klar hervorgehen. Doch sein Wesen birgt mehr als nur die Anziehungskraft der sichtbaren Dinge. Das schwedische Volk ist ein einsames Volk. Der Großteil der Bewohner ist nur durch eine Generation vom Leben auf dem Lande und von der jahrhundertelangen Isolierung in den Wäldern getrennt. Dies macht sie in einer Art und Weise scheu, die den Ausländer manchmal zu Unrecht dazu führt, sie als verschlossen und stolz zu bezeichnen. Es macht sie aber zugleich naiv und beinahe pathetisch interessiert an der Außenwelt und an der Meinung, die die Fremden über sie haben. Wenn sie ihre Scheu überwinden, überschütten sie den Besucher mit einer beunruhigenden Flut von Fragen. Mißgunst hat schon so manchen Ausländer dazu geführt, über die Schweden und ihr Land Dinge zu sagen oder zu schreiben, die nicht völlig der Wahrheit entsprechen. Die Schweden sind außerordentlich empfindlich für Kritik und wollen unbedingt sicher sein, daß sie das Rechte tun. Durch den Wohlstand und die Behaglichkeit, die das Ergebnis ihres gesunden Menschenverstandes in der Außenpolitik sind, fühlen sie sich von den Völkern weniger glücklicher Länder abgeschnitten, und dies gibt ihnen manchmal ein Gefühl der Schuld. Das ist bedauernswert, denn ohne sich dessen bewußt zu sein, haben sie ein Beispiel für die Zukunft gegeben. Es wäre allerdings töricht, wollte man unterstellen, daß dieses Beispiel keinerlei Nachteile aufweist.

Die Konzentration auf eine Friedenspolitik hat eine neue Art Menschen, den Friedensmenschen, geschaffen, und die Sozialpolitik der Regierung hat eher einen Preis für Intelligenz denn für Geburtsrang oder Reichtum ausgesetzt. Diese Konzentration bringt jedoch eine gewisse Gemessenheit und einen Mangel an Vitalität mit sich. Wenn der Ausländer auch mit Vergnügen feststellt, daß es im Alltag Schwedens nichts Vulgäres gibt, so mangelt es andererseits doch wieder an Schwung. Wer seinen Urlaub in Nachtlokalen zu verbringen gedenkt, möge lieber fernbleiben. Es gibt weder Jazz noch Gröhlen bei einem Aufenthalt in Schweden.

Ein unvergleichlicher Reiz ist diesem Lande eigen, und seine Ausdehnung führt zu gewaltigen Kontrasten. Während die Einwohner von Malmö oder Stockholm ein Leben führen, das dem in den anderen Städten Europas gleicht, züchten die Lappen, die in den nördlichen Provinzen wohnen, noch immer Rentiere, wie sie es jahrhundertelang taten. Selbst in den Städten ist die Erinnerung an das Landleben und die Landbräuche nach wie vor sehr stark; so werde ich nie den ungewöhnlichen Anblick der Teer- und Pechfackeln vergessen, die mit ihrem Schein von den Balkons der zentralgeheizten Wohnungen Stockholms das Neue Jahr grüßen. An Festtagen schütteln die Schweden ihre frischerworbenen städtischen Lebensformen ab und kehren zum Lande zurück. Im Hochsommer zum Beispiel scheint es, als würden sie aus den Städten ganz verschwinden, und der Ausländer kann sich glücklich preisen, wenn es ihm gelingt, sie ausfindig zu machen. Sie tanzen dann gewöhnlich um den Mittsommerbaum, wie es ihre Ahnen taten, bevor das Christentum nach Norden kam. Bei solchen Gelegenheiten erkennt man, daß sie durch den Aufbau und die Entwicklung der Städte nicht so viel von ihrem ursprünglichen Wesen verloren haben, wie mancher oberflächliche Beobachter meinen könnte.

Die schwedische Hausfrau kann in ihrer modern eingerichteten Küche unter Bedingungen arbeiten, die eines Millionärs würdig wären; dennoch wird sie Stunden damit verbringen, ein traditionelles Mahl zuzubereiten. Großkaufhäuser und Restaurants mit Selbstbedienung sind fester Bestandteil des täglichen Lebens. Aber man findet noch immer nichts dergleichen wie Standardbrot. Es gibt unzählige Variationen im Geschmack und in der Zusammensetzung von schwedischem Brot. Auch die Zubereitung und Aufbewahrung von Fisch wird in den verschiedensten Arten gehandhabt. Obwohl im Norden die Speisen sehr gesalzen werden, da das Schmelzwasser keine Mineralsalze enthält, gibt es doch wenig in der schwedischen Küche, was den Ausländer erschrecken lassen müßte. Der Heikle wird vielleicht besser keinen faulen Hering essen, der als große Delikatesse betrachtet wird; der Feinschmecker hinwiederum sollte die letzten zwei Augustwochen der Languste widmen, die beinahe Gegenstand allgemeiner Verehrung ist.

Verehrung ist vielleicht ein zu kräftiger Ausdruck gegenüber Langusten; er ist jedoch sicherlich nicht zu gewichtig für das Gefühl, das die schwedische Landschaft erweckt. Der Sommerhimmel dort birgt so etwas wie eine Vorahnung der Ewigkeit. Ich habe Momente erlebt, in denen ich fühlte, daß Schweden beinahe zu schön ist. Die Landschaft stört nie und behindert nie den Blick. Sie enthält immer eine Andeutung, als ob etwas unmittelbar hinter dem sichtbaren Horizont verborgen wäre. Selbst in den Städten spürt man den Duft der Nadelbäume, hört man den Nachklang des Waldesrauschens. Man fühlt sich entspannt und frei. Man teilt auch für kurze Zeit die Erfahrung der Schweden, das Bewußtsein, daß der Mensch schrecklich allein ist und daß er viel kleiner ist, als sein lärmendes Gehabe oft glauben lassen möchte. Es ist etwas zur Bescheidenheit Mahnendes in der schwedischen Landschaft, etwas gleichzeitig Entspannendes und Belebendes. Es ist etwas in ihr, das einen aufjauchzen macht über so viel Schönheit und das man doch nur sehr schwer in Worte kleiden kann. Ein Land wie Schweden bedarf keiner Worte. Man muß es sehen. Es verschließt den Mund und öffnet die Augen.

Skåne: an old street in Ystad
Skåne: une vieille rue à Ystad
Skåne: alte Straße in Ystad

Half-timbered houses in Ystad
Maisons à moitié en bois à Ystad
Fachwerkhäuser in Ystad

Skåne is a province of castles: Trollenäs Castle
Skåne est une région de châteaux: le château de Trollenäs
Skåne ist eine Provinz der Schlösser: Schloß Trollenäs

Vrams Gunnarstorp Castle
Le château de Vrams Gunnarstorp
Schloß Vrams Gunnarstorp

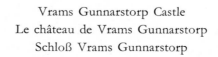

A street in Båstad
Une rue à Båstad
Straße in Båstad

The 14th century astronomical clock in the cathedral at Lund
L'horloge astronomique du XIVe siècle de la cathédrale de Lund
Astronomische Uhr aus dem 14. Jahrhundert in der Kathedrale zu Lund

The 11th century portal of the cathedral
Le portail du XIe siècle de la cathédrale
 Das aus dem 11. Jahrhundert stammende Portal der Kathedrale

Spring comes to a Skåne farm
Le printemps arrive à une ferme du Skåne
Der Frühling hält seinen Einzug in einem Bauerngut in Skåne

Endless sand on the south-west coast
Le sable à l'infini sur la côte sud-ouest
Endloser Sand an der Südwestküste

The moat of Trolle-Ljungby Castle
Le fossé du château de Trolle-Ljungby
Schloßgraben von Trolle-Ljungby

Blekinge: the harbour at Karlshamn
Blekinge: le port de Karlshamn
Blekinge: der Hafen von Karlshamn

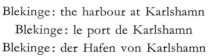

Småland: Kalmar Castle
Småland: le château de Kalmar
Småland: Schloß Kalmar

The medieval church at Hagby

L'église médiévale de Hagby

Die mittelalterliche Kirche in Hagby

Jönköping on Lake Vättern
Jönköping, sur le lac Vättern
Jönköping am Vättern-See

A summer festival in Halland
En été, un festival à Halland
Sommerfest in Halland

Cattle on the island of Öland
Bétail dans l'île de Öland
Rinder auf der Öland-Insel

Old barns at Glömminge
Vieilles granges a Glömminge
Alte Scheunen in Glömminge

Interior of a medieval church
Intérieur d'une église médiévale
Innenraum einer mittelalterlichen Kirche

Gotland: the city wall of Visby
Gotland: la muraille de la ville de Visby
Gotland: die Stadtmauer von Visby

Another part of the wall
Une autre partie de la muraille
An anderer Stelle der Stadtmauer

Feeding the chickens
Les poulets mangent ...
Hühnerfütterung

Visby, ruins of St Nicholas' monastery
Visby: ruines du monastère St. Nicolas
Visby, Ruinen des Klosters St. Nicolas

Detail of the ruins
Détail des ruines
Teilansicht der Ruinen

 47

Bohuslän: stock-fish being dried on the wharf at Klädesholmen
Bohuslän: morues séchant sur les quais à Klädesholmen
Bohuslän: Stockfisch dörrt auf dem Kai in Klädesholmen

'The Whale', an interesting rock formation at Lysekil
«La Baleine», curieux ensemble rocheux à Lysekil
„Der Wal", eine interessante Gesteinsbildung in Lysekil

Fishing boats at Smögen
Bateaux de pêche à Smögen
Fischerboote in Smögen

 Part of the Bohuslän archipelago
Une partie de l'archipel Bohuslän
Teilansicht des Inselmeers von Bohuslän

Svinesund, between Sweden and Norway
Le Svinesund, entre la Suède et la Norvège
Svinesund, zwischen Schweden und Norwegen

One of the canals in Gothenburg
Un des canaux de Gothenbourg
Einer der Kanäle in Göteborg

The old part of Gothenburg
Le vieux quartier de Gothenbourg
Das alte Göteborg

A fountain in one of Gothenburg's streets
Une fontaine dans l'une des rues de Gothenbourg
Springbrunnen in einer der Straßen Göteborgs

The harbour at Gothenburg, Scandinavia's largest port
Le port de Gothenbourg, le plus important des pays scandinaves
Der Hafen von Göteborg, der größte in Skandinavien

A pleasure boat in the harbour
Un bateau de plaisance dans le port
Vergnügungsboot im Hafen

Another view of the harbour
Une autre vue du port
Andere Hafenansicht

A boat in the harbour
Un bateau dans le port
Schiff im Hafen

Children playing among the boats
Enfants jouant parmi les bateaux
Spielende Kinder bei den Booten

Fishing smacks
Bateaux de pêche
Fischerboote

Walking along the quay
Promenade le long des quais
Promenade am Kai

Vadstena Convent Church in Östergötland
La chapelle du couvent de Vadstena dans l'Östergötland
Die Klosterkirche von Vadstena in Östergötland

Madonna in Vadstena Convent Church
Madone dans la chapelle du couvent de Vadstena
Madonna in der Klosterkirche von Vadstena

Vadstena Castle
Le château de Vadstena
Schloß Vadstena

A Runic stone at Rok

Pierre runique à Rok

Runenstein in Rok

 Swedish red-and-white cattle grazing on the Närke plains
Bétail suédois paissant dans les plaines de Närke
Schwedische Rinder auf der Weide in der Närke-Ebene

At work in a ceramic factory near Stockholm
Au travail dans une usine de céramique près de Stockholm
Bei der Arbeit: in einer Keramikfabrik bei Stockholm

A traditional Swedish Christmas dinner
Un dîner de Noël suédois traditionnel
Ein traditionelles schwedisches Weihnachtsmahl

Varnhem Abbey church in Västergötland
Eglise de l'abbaye de Varnhem dans le Västergötland
Die Abteikirche von Varnhem in Västergötland

An old windmill near Stockholm
Un vieux moulin à vent près de Stockholm
Alte Windmühle bei Stockholm

Regatta at Saltsjöbaden
Régates à Saltsjöbaden
Regatta in Saltsjöbaden

Bathing near Stockholm
Baignade près de Stockholm
Badefreuden in der Nähe von Stockholm

Summer houses in the Stockholm archipelago
Villas d'été dans l'archipel de Stockholm
Sommerhäuser auf den Inseln vor Stockholm

A boat in the archipelago
Un bateau dans l'archipel
Ein Schiff im Inselmeer

Boating near Stockholm
Canotage près de Stockholm
Bootsfahrt in der Nähe von Stockholm

A fortress in the archipelago
Une forteresse dans l'archipel
Festung auf einer der Inseln

Stockholm, Skansen

Ice-yachts at Djursholm
Bateaux à patins à Djursholm
Segelschlitten in Djursholm

Old wooden houses in Stockholm
Vieilles maisons en bois à Stockholm
Alte Holzhäuser in Stockholm

A quiet street
Une rue tranquille
Eine stille Straße

A modern school for girls in Stockholm
Une école moderne de jeunes filles à Stockholm
Moderne Mädchenschule in Stockholm

The Western Bridge
Le Pont de l'Ouest
Die Westbrücke

Modern flats in Stockholm
Appartements modernes à Stockholm
Moderne Wohnungen in Stockholm

More blocks of flats
D'autres immeubles d'appartements
Wohnblocks

The circular town hall at Gustafsberg
L'Hôtel de ville circulaire de Gustafsberg
Das runde Rathaus in Gustafsberg

The office buildings of the Co-operative Union
Le bâtiment des bureaux de l'Union des coopérateurs
Die Bürogebäude des Genossenschaftsverbandes

A little girl at the festival of Santa Lucia
Une petite fille au festival de Santa Lucia
Kleines Mädchen auf dem Fest der heiligen Lucia

Flats at Reymersholme
Appartements à Reymersholme
Wohnungen in Reymersholme

The open-air museum of Carl Milles, the famous sculptor
Le musée de plein air de Carl Milles, le fameux sculpteur
Das Freiluftmuseum des berühmten Bildhauers Carl Milles

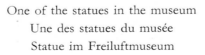

One of the statues in the museum
Une des statues du musée
Statue im Freiluftmuseum

Another statue in the 'Millesgården'
Une autre statue dans le «Millesgården»
Anderes Standbild im „Millesgården"

Statues at the water's edge
Statues au bord de l'eau
Statuen am Rande des Wassers

A statue among the tree tops
Une statue parmi les cîmes des arbres
Figuren zwischen den Baumwipfeln

A view of the museum
Une vue de musée
Teilansicht des Museums

A fountain in the museum
Une fontaine dans le musée
Springbrunnen im Museum

Detail of the fountain
Détail de la fontaine
Detail des Springbrunnens

One of the monuments in the King's Gardens, Stockholm
Un des monuments dans les jardins royaux
Eines der Denkmäler im Königsgarten, Stockholm

The Molin fountain in the King's Gardens
La fontaine Molin dans les jardins royaux
Der Molin-Springbrunnen im Königsgarten

Berzelius Park
Le parc Berzelius
Berzelius-Park

Fishing on a little island in the old quarter
Pêche dans une petite île du vieux quartier
Fischfang auf einer kleinen Insel im alten Stadtteil

A narrow street in the old town
Une rue étroite de la vieille ville
Schmale Gasse in der Altstadt

An open-air restaurant in Stockholm
Un restaurant en plein air à Stockholm
Eine Gaststätte im Freien

Modern flats in Kungsholmgatan
Appartements modernes à Kungsholmgatan
Moderne Wohnungen in Kungsholmgatan

A city street
Une rue de la cité
Straße in der Innenstadt

A cannon on the Royal Castle
Un canon sur le château royal
Geschütz auf dem Gelände des Königlichen Schlosses

On the old city island
Dans l'île de la vieille cité
Auf der Altstadtinsel

A ski-rack on the back of a Stockholm tram
Porte-skis à l'arrière d'un tramway de Stockholm
Skigestell an einer Stockholmer Straßenbahn

Parliament Square
Place du Parlement
Der Parlamentsplatz

The Royal Opera House
L'Opéra royal
Die Königliche Oper

The Hötorget Market
Le marché Hötorget
Der Hötorget-Markt

'Orpheus', the bronze statue outside the concert hall

«Orphée», groupe de bronze devant la salle de concerts

„Orpheus", Bronzestandbild vor dem Konzerthaus

The main figure of the statue
Personnage principal de la statue
Die Hauptfigur des Standbilds

One of Stockholm's rivers, with the Royal Opera House in the background
Une des rivières de Stockholm, avec l'Opéra royal à l'arrière-plan
Einer von Stockholms Wasserwegen; im Hintergrund die Königliche Oper

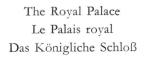

The Royal Palace
Le Palais royal
Das Königliche Schloß

The bridge leading to the Royal Palace
Le pont conduisant au Palais royal
Die Brücke zum Königlichen Schloß

The entrance to the House of Parliament
L'entrée du Parlement
Eingang zum Parlamentsgebäude

The façade of the Royal Palace seen from the north
La façade nord du Palais royal
Nordfassade des Königlichen Schlosses

Adrian de Vries statue at the Drottningholm Palace
La statue d'Adrian de Vries au palais de Drottningholm
Bronzestatue von Adrian de Vries, Schloß Drottningholm

Another of the statues
Une autre statue
Eine andere Statue

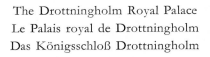

The Drottningholm Royal Palace
Le Palais royal de Drottningholm
Das Königsschloß Drottningholm

The palace and the gardens
Le palais et les jardins
Schloß und Park

The wrought-iron gates at the entrance to the palace
Les grilles en fer forgé de l'entrée du palais
Schmiedeeiserne Tore am Eingang zum Schloß

The Baroque portal of the cathedral in the old town

Le portail baroque de la cathédrale dans la vieille ville

Das Barockportal der Kathedrale in der Altstadt

The interior of the Riddarholm church where the Swedish kings are buried
L'intérieur de l'église Riddarholm où les rois de Suède sont enterrés
Innenansicht der Riddarholmskirche, Grabstätte der schwedischen Könige

Storkyrkan, the oldest church in Stockholm
Storkyrkan, la plus vieille église de Stockholm
Storkyrkan, die älteste Kirche Stockholms

Sunset in the Town Hall gardens
Coucher du soleil dans les jardins de l'Hôtel de ville
Sonnenuntergang im Stadthauspark

127

Evening
Soir
Abendstimmung

A statue in the Town Hall gardens
Une statue dans les jardins de l'Hôtel de ville
Statue im Stadthauspark

A fountain in the Town Hall gardens
Une fontaine dans les jardins de l'Hôtel de ville
Springbrunnen im Stadthauspark

130

The Town Hall, seen from the water

L'Hôtel de ville, vu du côté de l'eau

Das Stadthaus, vom Wasser aus gesehen

At the flower market
Au marché aux fleurs
Auf dem Blumenmarkt

Walking by the water
Promenade au bord de l'eau
Spaziergang am Wasser

The Palace Guard Band in the streets of Stockholm
La musique de la garde du palais dans les rues de Stockholm
Der Musikzug der Schloßgarde in den Straßen Stockholms

The band plays
La fanfare joue
Der Musikzug beim Spiel

Kungsgatan, Stockholm's main street, at night
Kungsgatan, rue principale de Stockholm, la nuit
Kungsgatan, Stockholms Hauptstraße, bei Nacht

The Royal Opera House in the evening
L'Opéra royal le soir
Die Königliche Oper am Abend

The city by night
La cité, la nuit
Die Stadt bei Nacht

A summer night on the Västerbro Bridge
Une nuit d'été sur le pont Västerbro
Eine Sommernacht auf der Västerbro-Brücke

The Slussen crossing
Le carrefour Slussen
Die Slussen-Kreuzung

A Stockholm street
Une rue de Stockholm
Straße in Stockholm

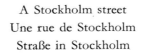

One of the archipelago steamers at the municipal wharf
Un des bateaux à vapeur de l'archipel au quai municipal
Einer der Inseldampfer am städtischen Landungsplatz

Sculpture on the quayside
Sculpture sur les quais
Bildwerk am Kai

'The City on the Water', seen from the Town Hall tower
«La cité sur l'eau» vue de la tour de l'Hôtel de ville
„Die Stadt auf dem Wasser", vom Stadthausturm aus gesehen

Tugs in the harbour
Remorqueurs dans le port
Schlepper im Hafen

Tourists on the Slussen quay
Touristes sur le quai Slussen
Touristen am Slussen-Kai

A view of Stockholm's quayside
Vue des quais de Stockholm
Blick auf Stockholms Kais

A moored excursion boat
Un bateau d'excursion amarré
Ein Ausflugsboot vor Anker

Waiting for the passengers
En attendant des passagers
In Erwartung der Passagiere

The harbour

Le port

Der Hafen

The harbour with the city in the background
Le port, avec la ville à l'arrière-plan
Hafenansicht mit Blick auf die Stadt

Tivoli, Stockholm's amusement park
Tivoli, le Luna-Park de Stockholm
Tivoli, Stockholms Vergnügungspark

One of the entertainments provided in the park
Une des attractions du parc
Eine der Vergnügungen des Parks

 The lights of Tivoli
Les lumières de Tivoli
Die Lichter Tivolis

155

One of Europe's first skyscrapers on Kungsgatan
Un des premiers gratte-ciels d'Europe dans la Kungsgatan
Einer der ersten Wolkenkratzer Europas in der Kungsgatan

The tower of the Town Hall, Stockholm's landmark
La tour de l'Hôtel de ville, point de répère de Stockholm
Der Stadthausturm, Stockholms Wahrzeichen

A bridge in Uppsala
Un pont à Uppsala
Brücke in Uppsala

Uppsala Cathedral
La cathédrale d'Uppsala
Die Domkirche von Uppsala

A quiet corner
Un coin tranquille
Ein stiller Winkel

A part of the cathedral
Une partie de la cathédrale
Teilansicht der Domkirche

Portal of the cathedral
Portail de la cathédrale
Portal der Domkirche

The river at Uppsala
La rivière à Uppsala
Uppsalas Fluß

Houses at the riverside
Maisons au bord de la rivière
Häuser am Flußufer

An Uppsala street
Une rue d'Uppsala
Straße in Uppsala

Uppsala's main square
La principale place d'Uppsala
Hauptplatz von Uppsala

The river

La rivière

Der Fluß

The Uppsala University
L'université d'Uppsala
Die Universität von Uppsala

In Uppsala
Dans Uppsala
In Uppsala

An old gateway leading to Uppsala Castle
Un vieux passage conduisant au château d'Uppsala
Alter Torweg zum Schloß von Uppsala

A corner of the Royal Castle
Un coin du château royal
Eckturm des Königsschlosses

A swimming pool in Uppsala
Une piscine à Uppsala
Schwimmbecken in Uppsala

 A Runic stone in Uppland
Une pierre runique à Uppland
Runenstein in Uppland

A farmstead in Värmland
Une ferme du Värmland
Gehöft in Värmland

The little town of Filipstad
La petite ville de Filipstad
Die kleine Stadt Filipstad

The forests of the Klarälven river valley
Les forêts de la vallée de la rivière Klarälven
Die Wälder des Klarälv-Tals

Modern flats in Karlskoga
Appartement modernes à Karlskoga
Moderne Wohnungen in Karlskoga

A traditional dance in central Sweden
Une danse traditionnelle en Suède centrale
Alter Volkstanz in Mittelschweden

A village church
Une église du village
Dorfkirche

Dalarna children
Enfants de Dalarna
Kinder in Dalarna

A young girl in traditional Dalarna folk costume
Une fillette en costume populaire folklorique de Dalarna
Junges Mädchen in der traditionellen Tracht von Dalarna

Snow in the Dalarna mountains
Neige sur les montagnes de Dalarna
Schnee in den Bergen von Dalarna

Skiers on a snowy path in Dalarna
Skieurs sur un sentier neigeux de Dalarna
Skifahrer auf einem schneebedeckten Pfad in Dalarna

A girl from Leksand with one of the traditional Dalarna horses
Une jeune fille de Leksand avec un des chevaux traditionnels de Dalarna
Mädchen aus Leksand mit einem der traditionellen Dalarna-Pferde

 A rowing competition with the old church boats on the Siljan lake
Une course d'aviron, avec les vieux bateaux folkloriques sur le lac Siljan
Ruderregatta der alten Kirchenboote auf dem Siljan-See

Ferrying across the river Dalälven
Passage en bac de la rivière Dalälven
Fähre über den Dalälv

The church at Rättvik

L'église à Rättvik

Die Kirche in Rättvik

Summer in the Härjedalen Highlands
Eté sur les hauteurs de Härjedalen
Sommer im Hochland von Härjedalen

Winter in the Härjedalen Highlands
Hiver sur les hauteurs de Härjedalen
Winter im Hochland von Härjedalen

A mountain dairy, used only during the summer months
Une laiterie de montagne, utilisée seulement les mois d'été
Sennerei in den Bergen

Crossing a mountain plateau along the marked track
En traversant un plateau montagneux le long d'un sentier marqué
Überquerung eines Bergplateaus entlang der Markierung

Forest scenery along the river Indalsälven in Medelpad
Paysage de forêt le long de la rivière Indalsälven à Medelpad
Waldlandschaft zu beiden Seiten des Indalsälv in Medelpad

Sleigh-riding in Jämtland
Partie de luge dans le Jämtland
Schlittenfahrt in Jämtland

Isolated village in Ångermanland
Village isolé dans le Ångermanland
Abgelegenes Dorf in Ångermanland

A row of modern houses in Kiruna
Une rangée de maisons modernes à Kiruna
Eine Reihe moderner Häuser in Kiruna

Lumberjacks at work
Bûcherons au travail
Holzfäller bei der Arbeit

Floating the logs down the river
Flottage
Abflößen der Baumstämme

A timber-assorting raft on a river in northern Sweden
Un train de bois sur une rivière dans le nord de la Suède
Floß auf einem Fluß in Nordschweden

An ore train on its way through Lappland
Un chargement de minerais traverse la Laponie
Ein Erzzug auf seinem Weg durch Lappland

A young Lapp girl
Une fillette laponne
Junges Lappenmädchen

An old Lapp woman
Une vieille femme laponne
Alte Lappenfrau

A Lapp boy looking out of his tent
Un garçon lapon regardant hors de sa tente
Lappenjunge im Zelteingang

A Lapp girl
Une jeune fille laponne
Lappenmädchen

Typical Norrland scenery
Scène typique du Norrland
Charakteristische Norrland-Landschaft

 Abiskojokk canyon in the mountains of Lappland
Les gorges de Abiskojokk dans les montagnes de Laponie
Abiskojokk-Cañon in den Bergen Lapplands

The Tarfala glacier in the Kebnekaise mountain region
Le glacier Tarfala dans la région montagneuse de Kebnekaise
Der Tarfala-Gletscher im Bergmassiv des Kebnekaise

A Lapplander with his reindeer
Un lapon et son renne
Ein Lappe mit seinem Ren

The mining town of Kiruna, within the Arctic Circle
La ville minière de Kiruna, au delà du cercle arctique
Die Bergwerksstadt Kiruna, nördlich des Polarkreises

The iron ore mountains at Kiruna
Les montagnes ferrugineuses de Kiruna
Die Eisenerzberge von Kiruna

The roaring torrents of the Abiskojokk river
Les torrents rugissants de la rivière Abiskojokk
Die donnernden Fluten des Abiskojokk

A reindeer herd
Une harde de rennes
Rentierherde

The cable-conveyor at Boliden gold mine
Le transporteur aérien à la mine d'or de Boliden
Transportseilbahn der Goldmine von Boliden

 213

A small village in southern Lappland
Un petit village en Laponie du sud
Kleines Dorf im Süden Lapplands

The ski-tow at Björkliden, which transports skiers to the mountain slopes

Le remonte-pente à Björkliden, qui transporte les skieurs vers les versants de la montagne

Skilift in Björkliden

Lapplanders
Lapons
Lappen

The National Park of Stora Sjöfallet

Le parc national de Stora Sjöfallet

Der Nationalpark von Stora Sjöfallet

Lake Sitojaure in the Sarek mountains
Le lac Sitojaure dans les montagnes de Sarek
Der Sitojaure-See im Gebirgsmassiv des Sarektjåkko

A skiing party approaching Mount Vassitjåkko
Un groupe de skieurs près du mont Vassitjåkko
Eine Gruppe von Skiläufern am Vassitjåkko

Winter light

Lumière d'hiver

Wintertag im Land der Mitternachtssonne

The midnight sun over Lake Torne Träsk

Le soleil de minuit sur le lac Torne Träsk

Mitternachtssonne über dem Torne-Träsk-See

A summer night in the mountains of Lappland
Une nuit d'été dans les montagnes laponnes
Sommernacht in den Bergen Lapplands

INDEX

✳

ACKNOWLEDGEMENTS

J. Allan Cash: cover photograph

Marco, Prague: 53—62, 71, 73—78, 80, 81, 83—86, 90—107, 110—114, 116—121, 123, 124, 127—137, 140—143, 146—169, 171—173, 181, 183, 220

Scandinavian Airlines System: 44, 46, 47, 68, 69, 109, 126, 178—180, 203, 204, 207

Swedish Tourist Traffic Association: 25—43, 45, 48—52, 63—67, 70, 72, 79, 82, 87—89, 108, 115, 122, 125, 138, 139, 144, 145, 170, 174—177, 182, 184—202, 205, 206, 208—219, 221, 222